My Anxiety Is Messing Things Up

TEACHER AND COUNSELOR ACTIVITY GUIDE

D1477884

BOYS TOWN Press
Boys Town, Nebraska

by Jennifer Licate

Illustrated by Suzanne Beaky

My Anxiety Is Messing Things Up Teacher and Counselor Activity Guide
Text and Illustrations Copyright © 2021 by Father Flanagan's Boys' Home
ISBN: 978-1-944882-90-7

Published by the Boys Town Press
13603 Flanagan Blvd.
Boys Town, NE 68010

All rights reserved under International and Pan-American Copyright Conventions. Unless otherwise noted, no part of this book may be reproduced, stored in a retrieval system, or transmitted in any form or by any means, electronic, mechanical, photocopying, recording or otherwise, without express written permission of the publisher, except for brief quotations or critical reviews.

For a Boys Town Press catalog, call **1-800-282-6657**
or visit our website: **BoysTownPress.org**

All Discussion Questions, Worksheets, and Activities are available for download.

ACCESS:
https://www.boystownpress.org/book-downloads

ENTER:
Your first and last names
Email address
Code: 944882mamtu907
Check "yes" to receive emails to ensure your email link is received.

Printed in the United States
10 9 8 7 6 5 4 3 2 1

Boys Town Press is the publishing division of Boys Town, a national organization serving children and families.

Table of Contents

Chapter 1

I'M OSCAR. MOST PEOPLE THINK I HAVE A LOT GOING FOR ME. I get good grades. Last year, my friend and I even won second place in our school's science fair. I also play on my school's baseball team and in the school band. I know a lot of kids, am pretty well-liked by everyone, and have been friends with the same group of guys for years.

I try my best in everything I do, which makes me look like a really responsible kid. But what most people don't know is that I put a lot of pressure on myself to excel. Sometimes it stresses me out. My parents also expect a lot from me. They don't think they do, but I feel the pressure. My older brother gets almost all A's in school. SO, I FEEL LIKE I HAVE TO DO THE SAME.

My parents say I'm a perfectionist. That basically means I try to do everything perfectly, which is impossible. I'm rarely satisfied with my best, and I'm always pushing myself to do things better.

I try not to be a perfectionist because it's too much pressure. I tell myself to just do the best I can. Sometimes that works. But mostly I feel the weight of all the expectations, pressure, and worry. Sometimes I think I feel fine when, suddenly, I notice I'm clenching my jaw or shoulders because I'm so anxious or trying to be perfect.

I usually can keep pretty calm during school because I'm busy and distracted. I'm most anxious when I try to go to sleep at night. My mind races with all the what ifs. What if I didn't study enough for the test? What if I fail the test? What if I fail the class? That would make my parents so mad...What if I flunk out of school?

Deep down, I know most of these what ifs will never happen and I should stop worrying. Still, it's hard for me to relax. My heart races and my body gets all jittery, making it hard to fall asleep. The longer it takes to fall asleep the more frustrated I get, which stresses me out even more. I GET SO RESTLESS, SOME NIGHTS I'M UP UNTIL 2 OR 3 IN THE MORNING!

I try to put off going to bed, hoping I'll be so tired that I'll fall asleep as soon as my head hits the pillow. Unfortunately, it hasn't worked yet.

Most mornings, I wake up exhausted and cranky. It's hard to be in a good mood when I'm tired day after day. I try to give myself a pep talk as I get ready. I say to myself today will be better, and I'll be relaxed enough to get some sleep tonight and feel better.

This morning, I'm in a bad mood again. When I got to school, I hung with my friends before class started, like I normally do. But I didn't really want to talk or hang out. I just wanted to get the day over with so I could go home and chill. I stood emotionless while my friends laughed and joked around. Darius looked at me, somewhat confused. "What's up with you, dude?" he asked.

"NOTHING!" I SNAPPED. "You guys just aren't funny. It's the same stupid jokes every day."

"Oh, my bad," Jayden said in his snarkiest voice. "Next time we'll try to keep you entertained." Then the bell rang. My friends grabbed their bookbags and walked off to class. Why did I do that, I wondered? Ugh, I always do that! Why can't I just keep my mouth shut and not start a fight? I can't believe I went off on my friends. Now I have another thing to worry about, friends hating me. WHAT A TERRIBLE WAY TO START THE DAY!

CHAPTER ONE

Follow Up Discussion Questions and Activities

Discussion Questions

1. Have you ever felt pressure to do well in school? Or in activities?

- Do you put pressure on yourself?

- Does the pressure come from someone/somewhere else?

2. Have you ever felt worried or anxious?

© 2022 Father Flanagan's Boys' Home

3. What situations cause kids to feel worried or anxious?

4. Have you heard the term "perfectionist" before?

- What do you think perfectionist means?

5. Do you ever get mad at yourself for how you talk to friends when you're in a bad mood?

6. Do you ever get mad at yourself for how you talk to teachers, parents, or other adults when you're in a bad mood?

Activities

Exploring Anxiety Activity

1. Ask students: What situations do you think cause kids the most anxiety?
2. Write all situations on the front board.
3. Instruct students to vote.
4. Place students into groups based on their vote.
5. Explain to the small groups: As a group, list the reasons why you think the situation you chose causes anxiety.
6. Give groups about 15 minutes to list their reasons.
7. Explain to group: This exercise shows the many situations that cause worry or anxiety in kids your age. You don't always know who is experiencing anxiety and worry. Be sensitive to others in these situations.

Notes:

© 2022 Father Flanagan's Boys' Home

MY ANXIETY IS MESSING THINGS UP

SETTING YOUR DAILY MANTRA ACTIVITY WORKSHEET

Think of a situation that causes you to worry or feel anxious. Write down what you can say to yourself as a pep talk to go into that situation with a more positive mindset.

STRUGGLE	PEP TALK

Notes:

TEACHER AND COUNSELOR ACTIVITY GUIDE

Chapter 2

SNAPPING AT MY FRIENDS PUT ME IN AN AWFUL FUNK. I WAS IN CLASS, STARING AT THE CLOCK, WAITING FOR THE BELL TO RING. I SHOULD'VE BEEN LISTENING TO MY MATH TEACHER, BUT I COULDN'T CONCENTRATE. IT WAS ALMOST LUNCHTIME, AND I WAS WORRIED ABOUT MEETING UP WITH MY FRIENDS. WOULD THEY STILL BE MAD AT ME? I know I was a jerk this morning, but I didn't mean it. I was just in a bad mood because I was so tired.

Lunch is usually the best part of my day, and not just because I'm usually starving and the food is good. It's fun to hang out with the guys and joke around. I don't usually joke or talk too much in class because I don't want to get in trouble. I hate when my teachers are disappointed in me. Plus, I'm always worried they'll message my parents. It's even worse when my parents are upset with me. Man, I hope this morning's incident won't make lunch messy too.

AT LAST, THE BELL FINALLY GOES OFF! I SHOVE ALL MY BOOKS INTO MY BOOKBAG AND START HEADING OUT OF CLASS WHEN MS. LOPEZ STOPS ME.

"Oscar, can you wait a minute?" she asked, as I tried to speed past her.

"Sure," I said with a tinge of hesitation. I knew when Ms. Lopez asked me to stay, it wasn't really a question. It was more of a command. I leaned against her desk and waited for the rest of the kids to pack up and leave. All I wanted to do was get to lunch. What did Ms. Lopez need to talk to me about anyway?

Once the classroom cleared out, Ms. Lopez stared at me and asked, "Oscar, you seemed distracted during class. IS EVERYTHING OKAY?" Did she notice that I was worried? Can everyone tell that I'm worried? My mind filled with self-doubt. "I'm okay. I'm just anxious to see my friends because I was kinda rude this morning, and I don't want them to be mad."

"It can be tough to face someone when you've made a mistake," she said. "But it's good you recognized the mistake, so you can apologize and make it better."

I tugged on the straps of my backpack and stared at my shoes. "Yeah, I just hope it works. It would be bad if my friends didn't want to hang out with me anymore or if I ruined lunch for everyone."

"I bet if you address it the right way, it will all work out. Do you often get worried or stressed about things, Oscar?"

"Ugh..." I mumbled.

How am I supposed to answer? What's the right answer? I don't want her to think I'm anxious all the time and there's something messed up with me. But if I'm being honest, I do get anxious a lot.

"OSCAR, IT'S OKAY IF YOU GET STRESSED AND NEED SOME HELP DEALING WITH IT," Ms. Lopez assured me. "You're such a good student, and sometimes keeping up with schoolwork can be stressful."

I was relieved she understood. After an awkwardly long pause, I admitted the truth. "Yeah, I guess I do feel like I need help sometimes."

"You know, Oscar, Mrs. Wang is restarting a

counseling group for kids to meet and talk about ways to deal with anxiety. She's run the group before, and it's great. I could ask her to talk to you, if you think you'd be interested in joining?"

"Mrs. Wang, the school counselor?"

"Yes, she's really easy to talk to and helps a lot of students."

I don't care how easy she is to talk to, I don't want anyone to know I'm anxious. What will everyone think?

"I don't know, Ms. Lopez," I said, as I searched for any excuse to shut this conversation down and get to lunch. But she persisted. "Let me tell her you may be interested, and she can explain the group to you. You can always say no."

"Okay, I guess so," I said, knowing I was never joining a group like that.

"GREAT! I'll let you get to your next class. Do you need a pass?"

"No, I'm just going to lunch."

"Okay, bye Oscar!"

"Bye," I said and nervously hurried off to the cafeteria.

By the time I went through the lunch line and got to my usual table, all my buddies were laughing and finishing their lunch.

"What's up?" I asked, pretending like my morning freak out never happened.

"Hey Oscar," Michael answered, while offering a fist bump.

"We didn't know where you were," said Darius.

"We thought you stormed outta school cause you were all mad about something," Jayden joked.

"Yeah, sorry about this morning guys."

"No worries, dude. We're used to it," laughed Darius, as he sucked the last drop of milk from the carton.

I was so relieved they weren't mad at me. But did Darius just say they're used to it? That must mean I'm cranky a lot. I thought I was hiding my bad moods. MAYBE I DO NEED HELP DEALING WITH MY ANXIETY.

CHAPTER 2

Follow Up Discussion Questions and Activities

Discussion Questions

1. Do you have a favorite part of your school day?

2. What emotions do you think Oscar felt while talking to Ms. Lopez?

- Why do you think he felt that way?

3. What are the benefits of joining a counseling group at school?

- Are there any risks in joining a counseling group at school?

4. After Oscar talked to Ms. Lopez, do you think he was interested in joining Mrs. Wang's group?

© 2022 Father Flanagan's Boys' Home

5. Did Oscar handle the argument with his friends well?

    - How else could he have handled the situation? Give examples.

6. Were you surprised that Oscar's friends were not mad at him?

    - Why or why not?

7. Has Oscar's opinion about joining Mrs. Wang's group changed?

    - If yes, what caused his opinion to change?

Activities

Writing Activity

1. Explain to students that they will write a journal entry from the perspective of one of Oscar's friends (Darius, Jayden, or Michael).
2. Ask students to consider: How does the friend view Oscar and his behavior? How did Oscar's bad mood make him feel? When Oscar apologized for his behavior, his friends told him they were used to it. How did the friend feel now? Has the friend's view of Oscar changed?
3. Allow students about 15-20 minutes to complete their journal entries during class.
4. Encourage group discussion by asking students: Would anyone like to share their journal entry, or parts of it with the group? What are some possible consequences if Oscar continues to act in this way?

Exploring Options Activity

1. Discuss with students: Ms. Lopez suggested Oscar join Mrs. Wang's counseling group to deal with anxiety. Do you think Oscar should join the group?
   - Why or why not?
2. Divide students into two groups based on if they think Oscar should join the group or not.
3. Explain to students: Small groups will focus on either creating a list of the possible benefits of joining the counseling group or the possible risks of joining the group. Each group should pick a representative to share their list with the larger group.
4. Give groups about 15-20 minutes to brainstorm a list of reasons to support their position.
5. Ask students: Now that you have heard all the reasons Oscar should and should not join the group, do you think Oscar should join the group? Has your opinion changed based on the discussion?

© 2022 Father Flanagan's Boys' Home

MY ANXIETY IS MESSING THINGS UP

EXPLORING OPTIONS ACTIVITY WORKSHEET

Do you think Oscar should join the group? Why or why not?

____

____

____

Make a list below.

Benefits of Joining	Reasons for Not Joining

Chapter 3

A few days later, I was feeling tired again. I had another bad night of sleep because of my anxiety. In Spanish class, Mr. Charles had just announced we could work on our homework when the classroom phone rang, startling everyone and making us all curious.

"Sí, I'll send him right down," Mr. Charles said into the phone. The whole class held its breath, anxiously waiting to hear which unlucky kid was about to be sent down to the principal's office. I wondered what they did. Probably nothing good.

Mr. Charles hung up and turned toward me. "Oscar, pack up your books and come here."

I could feel everyone's eyes on me. My face felt warm and flushed. I hate being the

CENTER OF ATTENTION. IT'S SO EMBARRASSING!

Why am I being called to the office? I can't remember doing anything wrong.

I packed up my books as fast as I could and walked toward Mr. Charles. He looked at me with a blank expression and whispered, "Oscar, Mrs. Wang, the school counselor, wants to see you. Please go to her office now."

I said okay and walked out.

I've never been to the counselor's office. I only know Mrs. Wang because she comes into my classes sometimes. She teaches us about topics like bullying prevention and having a growth mindset. I was feeling nervous when I got to her office.

Mrs. Wang greeted me with much more enthusiasm than I expected.

"Please sit down, Oscar, and we can chat."

I sat down across from her, in a chair that was surprisingly comfortable.

"Oscar, Ms. Lopez shared with me that you've been feeling stressed. CAN WE TALK ABOUT WHAT'S STRESSING YOU OUT?" Mrs. Wang's voice was warm and reassuring.

"Umm... I guess lots of things. Grades.

Sports. Parents. Friends."

My answers hung in the air for a moment before Mrs. Wang spoke. "That does seem like a lot to worry about. You mentioned your parents. Do you feel like they're unhappy with you or disappointed in you?"

I shook my head no. To be honest, I probably should have nodded yes.

"They always say they want me to try my best, but my brother is super smart. My best and his best are really different. I just don't wanna be the one who always disappoints them," I said.

"It sounds like you're feeling a lot of pressure to keep up with your brother and meet your parents' expectations. I think you'd really benefit from joining the counseling group for students struggling with stress and anxiety. It's called the Coping with Anxiety & Taming Stress Group. But, that's too long. CATS is our fun nickname."

I don't want to join a counseling group, even one with a fun nickname. But, I didn't want to hurt her feelings.

"The group is made up of students your age who are feeling stressed. In group, we'll talk about what causes stress and strategies to help you deal with it," she explained. "Everyone needs strategies to manage their stress, and this group will teach you several different ones you can use."

I DO NEED TO LEARN HOW TO DE-STRESS, I GUESS. I wanna be able to sleep and not feel so worried all the time. Maybe the group isn't such a bad idea?

"Who's in the group, Mrs. Wang?"

"Well Oscar, I can't tell you who will be in the group because that's confidential right now. But, if you do decide to join the group, you must agree to follow an important rule."

"Every student must agree that anything said during group cannot be repeated to other kids who aren't in group. Privacy is important. I want everyone to feel safe to share their feelings. There will be other group rules once we start meeting, but members get to have a say in those. We will meet during resource period, so you won't miss any class time. I know missing class can cause students more stress, so I try to avoid that as much as possible."

"I THINK I'D LIKE TO JOIN THE GROUP!" The words flew out of my mouth before my mind had a chance to say shut up. I surprised myself... never thought I'd agree to join.

"THAT'S AWESOME," Mrs. Wang excitedly declared. "The group meets every Wednesday, and I'll give you a pass on Wednesday morning so you'll know to come to my office during resource period."

"Okay, sounds good, Mrs. Wang."

She was really excited to have me in the group, and she assured me it would make a difference. She told me I could stop by any time if I had questions or wanted to chat, and then she handed me my hall pass and wished me a great rest of the day.

CHAPTER 3

Follow Up Discussion Questions and Activities

Discussion Questions

1. What emotions do you think Oscar felt when he was called to the counselor's office?

- Why was he feeling this way?

2. Have you ever been called to the counselor's office?

- Do you feel like you're in trouble when you're called to the counselor's office?

© 2022 Father Flanagan's Boys' Home

3. Oscar named a number of things that caused him stress. Do you think a lot of kids your age stress over the same things?

4. Would missing class stress you out?

- Is it hard to catch up when you miss class?

5. Were you surprised Oscar decided to join the CATS Group?

- Why do you think Oscar decided to join the CATS Group?

Activities

Art Activity

1. Explain to students: Oscar talked to Mrs. Wang about the CATS Group. During their conversation, Oscar changed his mind from not wanting to join the group to agreeing to join. Draw a picture of Oscar and write down what you think his thoughts were during their conversation. What thoughts do you think made him change his mind?
2. Give students a few minutes to do this activity.
3. Divide students into pairs.
4. Instruct students: Share your drawings and thoughts with your partner.
5. After giving students the necessary time to share, ask students: Would anyone like to share?

Brainstorming Activity

1. Explain to students: Mrs. Wang stated that group rules are created at the start of group and one of the most important rules is confidentiality.
2. Divide students into groups of 3-4 students.
3. Tell students, as a group discuss:
   - What does confidentiality mean to you?
   - Are there any other rules that are important for a counseling group of students?
4. Allow groups about 10 minutes to brainstorm.
5. Ask groups: Who would like to share their definition of confidentiality and/or group rules with the class?
   - Why do you think that rule is important?

© 2022 Father Flanagan's Boys' Home

MY ANXIETY IS MESSING THINGS UP

DRAWING WORKSHEET

Draw a picture of Oscar and write down what you think his thoughts were during his conversation with Mrs. Wang.

Notes:

TEACHER AND COUNSELOR ACTIVITY GUIDE

Chapter 4

I felt better after my chat with Mrs. Wang, but I was still anxious. At night, my head was full of worry, and I couldn't shut it out. I told my mom about Mrs. Wang's group. She was excited for me, hoping I'd learn some new strategies. Mom knows all about my struggles with anxiety. She suggested I listen to music to relax and sleep. I tried that, but it never helped much. Even when I play soothing music, I toss and turn for hours before falling asleep.

Today, I received my pass from Mrs. Wang to go to the CATS Group. I was relieved and a little excited to finally start. But I was nervous, too.

When it was time to meet, I walked into Mrs. Wang's office. All the chairs were arranged in a circle. I was one of the last to arrive so I grabbed one of the few available chairs.

I was next to Abby, who I recognized from one of my other classes. I didn't know anyone else but some faces looked familiar. None of my buddies were there, which I kinda expected. I hadn't talked to them about the group.

I don't know why. I know they'd be cool with me being in the group, but they'd probably ask a ton of questions. I had lots of questions myself and wouldn't be able to answer anyone else's. I DIDN'T KNOW WHAT THE CATS GROUP WOULD BE LIKE, I JUST HOPED IT'D HELP ME.

Mrs. Wang started the meeting by having each of us introduce ourselves, then we talked about the group rules. The first rule was that everyone has to be respectful when others are talking. You can't say anything mean or disrespectful, or tell someone their feelings are wrong. The second rule was about confidentiality. No one's allowed to talk about anything shared during group, outside of group. Mrs. Wang had all of us sign a sheet of paper, kind of like a contract, to show we agreed to follow the rules.

After all the introductions and formalities were done, Mrs. Wang explained what anxiety is and the different situations that can cause people to feel anxious. She asked for volunteers to share with the group what causes them anxiety. Nia went first.

I could tell she was nervous as she told us how tests make her stress out.

"I never sleep the night before tests, and then I'm so exhausted that it's almost impossible to get a good grade."

Hearing Nia admit to having sleep issues when she's anxious made me feel less alone. I wasn't the only one tossing and turning all night. I knew other people struggled with anxiety, BUT I NEVER HEARD SOMEONE MY AGE TALK ABOUT IT.

Next up was Zion, who talked about being anxious and worried that something bad will happen to his parents and sister. His mom was in a car accident when he was younger, and it was so bad that she was in intensive care for a while. Even though she's fine now, he worries she'll get in another accident. Zion said his anxiety, at first, was centered around his mom but now he worries about his dad and sister too. Anytime he's not with them, he's worried about them.

I volunteered to go next. I felt more comfortable after watching Nia and Zion be so open and honest.

"I get anxious about lots of things. I put a lot of pressure on myself to do well in everything...

sports, school. I hate when I disappoint my parents or when my friends are mad at me. I hate when anyone's mad at me. No matter what I do, I feel like I'm disappointing someone." I stopped and took a deep breath. "WHAT NIA SAID ABOUT SLEEP IS TRUE FOR ME. MY ANXIETY KEEPS ME AWAKE AT NIGHT, TOO."

Mrs. Wang, in a burst of excitement, clasped her hands together and declared, "SEE, THIS IS WHAT'S SO GREAT ABOUT OUR GROUP. WE CAN SUPPORT ONE ANOTHER BECAUSE WE HAVE SIMILAR STRUGGLES. THANK YOU FOR MAKING THAT CONNECTION, OSCAR."

Now it was José's turn. In a hushed tone that was barely above a whisper, he said, "I get anxious around other kids."

I'm fine with adults, but I get nervous talking to kids I don't know. I get nervous that I'm gonna say something stupid. Or if I try to be funny, but it won't be funny, and then everyone will just stop and stare at me. It's so hard to walk up to a group of kids who are already talking. Even if I'm friends with some of the kids, it makes me nervous."

Abby agreed and then chimed in. "I feel the same way. I hate when it feels like everyone's looking at me. I don't even like walking across the cafeteria to go to my lunch table. It feels like everyone's staring at me, waiting for me to trip or something."

José nodded in agreement.

Mrs. Wang thanked José and Abby for sharing and being supportive. "I'm glad to see another example of everyone supporting each other. It helps to know you're not the only one who's dealing with anxiety in these situations. The more you challenge yourself to face these stressful situations and see positive outcomes, or even neutral outcomes, the more confidence you'll have in dealing with similar situations in the future. Over time, this confidence will reduce your anxiety."

Everyone looked more relaxed and hopeful after Mrs. Wang's encouragement. I sure hope she's right, and I can learn how to reduce my anxiety through this group.

"Thanks for coming and participating, everyone. This is gonna be a great CATS group!" Mrs. Wang said. "Next time we meet, we'll talk about how anxiety affects our bodies and how it makes us feel."

CHAPTER 4

Follow Up Discussion Questions and Activities

Discussion Questions

1. How do you think Oscar felt when he didn't know anyone in the group?

2. Why do you think Oscar didn't tell his friends about the group?

3. How did the group members help to change Oscar's feelings from nervousness to excited and hopeful?

4. Were you surprised by the situations that made group members anxious?

- Would you feel anxious in similar situations?

© 2022 Father Flanagan's Boys' Home

5. How do you think group members felt when someone described an experience with anxiety that was very similar to their own experience?

____

____

____

____

____

6. Have you ever shared an upsetting experience with someone and then discovered they had a similar experience?

____

____

____

____

____

- How did it make you feel?

  ____

  ____

  ____

Activities

Exploring Anxiety Activity

1. Discuss with the group: Group members talked about the anxiety they felt in different situations. Do you ever feel anxious? If so, write about a time when you were anxious and the physical effects the anxiety created.
   - If you cannot think of a time you felt anxious, choose one of the group members (Nia, Zion, Josè, or Abby) and create a situation that would likely give them anxiety and describe how you think they would feel.
2. Advise students: This description of anxiety can be in any method you feel most comfortable; a short essay, a drawing, a bulleted list, etc.

Writing Activity

1. Discuss with the group: Mrs. Wang said, "The more you challenge yourself to face these stressful situations and see positive outcomes, or even neutral outcomes, the more confidence you'll have in dealing with similar situations in the future. Over time, this confidence will reduce your anxiety."
   - Do you agree or disagree with this statement?
   - Write why you agree or disagree, using any personal examples or experiences you have.
   - Have you ever intentionally placed yourself in a stressful situation to test yourself and your response? Was the outcome positive?
2. Allow students about 15-20 minutes to write their responses.
3. Ask students: Would anyone would like to share your opinion and/or experiences?

Notes:

© 2022 Father Flanagan's Boys' Home

MY ANXIETY IS MESSING THINGS UP

EXPLORING ANXIETY WORKSHEET

Write or draw about a time when you were anxious and the physical effects the anxiety created.

Notes:

TEACHER AND COUNSELOR ACTIVITY GUIDE

Chapter 5

Over the next few weeks, I grew more and more comfortable in group as I got to know everyone. I learned I wasn't the only kid dealing with the physical side effects of anxiety. Our anxiety may be triggered by different events or circumstances, but we all experienced physical symptoms. The most common physical symptoms the kids had were stomachaches, headaches, a racing heart, disrupted sleep, irritability, and a general feeling of jumpiness or restlessness.

During group, Nia described what it felt like to have an anxiety attack. She said she's only had one, and it happened while she was taking a big test. Ever since, she's become even more anxious because she doesn't ever want to feel like that again.

"All I can remember is my heart beating really fast and feeling like time stood still," Nia said.

"I wanted to run to the bathroom because I felt like I was gonna puke, but I couldn't move. I looked around the room and the other kids were acting normal. I KEPT THINKING, 'WHY IS NO ONE ELSE TOTALLY FREAKING OUT?'"

During another group meeting, we learned what happens inside our bodies when we feel anxious. When you're in a stressful situation, your body goes into fight, flight, or freeze mode. It responds as if it's in physical danger. You either want to fight, flight (run), or freeze (you're too afraid to move). Your body responds by releasing chemicals to get you out of the dangerous situation, not realizing the threat is only in your mind. These chemicals cause certain parts of your brain to slow down.

I learned there's a reason I can't remember anything when I'm anxious, AND IT MADE SO MUCH SENSE! When I'm anxious about giving a presentation or taking a test, it's harder to do well because I have trouble remembering what I studied. My brain and body are focused on keeping me safe from the danger. I really was learning a lot being in the CATS Group.

After a couple meetings talking about how anxiety makes us feel, Mrs. Wang said we were ready to move forward and focus on finding strategies to help us manage our anxiety.

FINALLY! THAT'S WHAT I'D BEEN WAITING FOR. I NEED TO LEARN HOW TO CALM MYSELF DOWN, SO I CAN SLEEP.

Mrs. Wang told us there are lots of strategies for managing anxiety, BUT NOT ALL OF THEM WILL WORK FOR EVERYONE.

"Some strategies will feel more comfortable for you, based on your personality and the types of situations that make you feel anxious," she said.

Mrs. Wang looked around the room, eyeing each of us to make sure we understood what she had said, then she continued.

"One strategy is physical exercise, but exercise will look different based on the situation. If you're feeling anxious at home, you could go for a walk, or a run, or do jumping jacks. But when you're feeling anxious in school, you can't just go run or jump up and down."

"Physical exercise might involve asking your teacher if you can be excused so you can walk to the hydration station or staying at your desk and doing chair push-ups."

I had no idea what chair push-ups were, and my confusion showed on my face. Confusion was on everyone's face.

"Do you not know what chair push-ups are?" Mrs. Wang asked us. In unison, a half-dozen heads shook to say no.

"OH, PERFECT! I'LL SHOW YOU."

Mrs. Wang then proceeded to demonstrate the chair push-up. She put her hands under the arms of her chair and then lifted her legs up and raised her body slightly out of the chair. "Now everyone try. Do you see how doing this could release some physical energy?" she asked.

Some of us nodded while others struggled to lift themselves up.

"THE IMPORTANT THING IS LEARNING WHAT STRATEGIES WORK FOR YOU."

"You can even have some strategies that work when you're alone and others that work when you're around people. You need to find and use strategies that work for you and whatever situations cause you stress."

Mrs. Wang then asked if any of us had found a stress-reducing strategy that works well. Naturally, none of us had one. That's probably why we're all here in the first place. Mrs. Wang said not to worry, she just wanted to check. Then she gave us a homework assignment to complete before next week's meeting.

"I want each of you to practice these two anxiety-reducing strategies and see how well they work. The first strategy is physical exercise. Each night this week, do some physical exercise. Go on a walk, do push-ups, or any physical activity you enjoy. THE SECOND STRATEGY I WANT YOU TO DO INVOLVES JOURNALING. I have journals for each of you. Every night, before bed, write down your thoughts. Write about what's bothering you, your plans for the next day, or whatever is on your mind. It doesn't have to be long, and you don't have to worry about proper punctuation or grammar. Can we all agree to try both of these strategies until we meet again next week?"

EVERYONE AGREED.

CHAPTER 5

Follow Up Discussion Questions and Activities

Discussion Questions

1. The group talked about some of the physical effects of anxiety. Are there any other physical effects that were not mentioned?

2. Did you learn anything new about anxiety from reading this chapter?

3. Were you surprised that Nia felt comfortable enough in group to share about her anxiety attack?

- What do you think made her feel comfortable enough to share?

4. Mrs. Wang discussed how physical exercise could be used as a strategy to deal with anxiety, but it may look different based on the situation. Can you think of another helpful strategy that can be modified or adjusted based on the situation?

© 2022 Father Flanagan's Boys' Home

6. No one in group shared any strategies they've used to deal with anxiety. Do you think it's because...

- Option 1: No one had any helpful strategies to share?

- Option 2: They were too nervous to share strategies with the group?

- Option 3: They didn't think the strategies they tried in the past would be helpful because they didn't work for them or were too complicated to explain?

7. Everyone agreed to try physical exercise and journaling over the next week to help them deal with their anxiety.

- Would you agree to try these strategies if you were in the group?

- What do you think would happen if someone refused to try one or both of these strategies?

Activities

Role-Play Activity

1. Remind the group that Nia described what it felt like to have an anxiety attack in the story.
2. Divide students into groups of 3-4.
3. Explain to students: Each group will write a short skit about someone your age who experiences an anxiety attack. The skit should include the following information:
   - The situation that leads to or causes the anxiety attack.
   - How he or she feels during the anxiety attack.
   - The physical symptoms he or she experiences.
   - The strategies he or she uses to deal with the anxiety attack.
   - If you aren't familiar with these symptoms and/or strategies you can research them online.
   - You will need to be prepared to act out your skit in front of the class.
4. Give each group about 15 to 20 minutes to develop their skit.

Personal Reflection Activity

1. Discuss with the group: Have you ever felt like your body went into fight, flight, or freeze mode when you were anxious?
2. Instruct students: Write a short story or draw a picture explaining that experience.
3. Give students about 15-20 minutes to work on their stories/drawings.
4. Afterwards, ask students if anyone would like to share their story or drawing.
5. Discuss:
   - What strategies did you use to deal with your anxiety?
   - Are there any additional strategies that would help reduce anxiety in this situation?

© 2022 Father Flanagan's Boys' Home

MY ANXIETY IS MESSING THINGS UP

PERSONAL REFLECTION ACTIVITY WORKSHEET

Have you ever felt like your body went into fight, flight or freeze mode when you were anxious? Write a short story or draw a picture of that experience.

Chapter 6

I was excited to try exercising and journaling. Over the next week, I did both every day. Even when it was cold, I rode my bike around the neighborhood after school or right after dinner. The first few days, it annoyed me that I had to exercise when all I really wanted to do was relax. Eventually, I started looking forward to the bike rides. Sometimes I'd listen to music as I biked, but other times I craved the silence. Biking gave me time to think through what was bothering me and what I could do to fix my problems. I was surprised that I always came home in a better mood after a ride.

I also journaled every night before bed. I basically wrote down what I thought about during my bike rides, plus questions I had about life and my future.

In the beginning, my attitude about journaling was similar to when I started biking. It was like a homework assignment that I struggled to complete. But after a while, I realized journaling was helping me. I liked getting my thoughts on paper. Before I started journaling, I had so many thoughts swimming around in my head. But now I have somewhere to leave them. I can come back to them whenever I want, and I'm not constantly distracted by trying to figure everything out.

I went into the next group session excited to share how both strategies helped me. Just knowing I had a plan to deal with my anxiety was a relief. I was finally having an easier time sleeping. I didn't fall asleep right away, but it didn't take as long as before.

Mrs. Wang was excited to see all of us and asked how our homework assignments went. Several of us said we liked it. Others just nodded their approval.

"GREAT! It looks like you all had a good experience. Would anyone like to share how these strategies affected their anxiety?" Mrs. Wang asked.

"How about you, Oscar? I heard you say you liked it."

"YEAH, I DID. I didn't expect to. At first I thought, 'Aargh, more homework,' because my schoolwork already gives me anxiety."

Some of the kids snickered and nodded because they understood homework anxiety. I smiled and continued, "But after a couple of days, I started looking forward to the assignments. I realized they were helping me feel calmer, less anxious."

"I'm so glad to hear it!" exclaimed Mrs. Wang. "How'd you sleep last week? Any better?"

"Yeah, it was a little better. I still had trouble getting to sleep, but I didn't feel as restless. And it took me less time to fall asleep."

"OSCAR, THAT'S GREAT! I'M SO HAPPY THE STRATEGIES HELPED YOU!"

Everyone had an opportunity to share how they liked journaling and exercising. Turns out, the strategies helped everyone. But some kids like doing one way more than the other.

José said he liked exercise better. In his journal, he just wrote a quick list of what happened during the day. But he spent as long as he could outside playing basketball or going for a run. The movement helped him clear his head.

ABBY WAS THE OPPOSITE. She liked journaling better. "I took my dog for short walks every afternoon, but I spent more time journaling," she said. "I journaled about everything. My day. How I felt when I talked to other kids in school, and what I want my future to be like."

"Journaling helped me realize I don't feel uncomfortable around all the kids at school, just the ones who seem like they're judging me."

"That's a great point, Abby! Sometimes journaling helps you understand what's really bothering you," said Mrs. Wang. "And now that you know, you can make changes for the better. You can put your energy into creating friendships with the kids you're comfortable around."

Abby agreed and then Mrs. Wang told her she seems really comfortable around the kids in our group.

"Yeah, I am. You're all really supportive, and I appreciate it. Thanks guys!" Abby said to all of us. Everyone smiled. Our CATS Group does support one another.

"I'm glad you all had a good experience with journaling and being physically active," said Mrs. Wang. "Next week is our LAST meeting ALREADY! Can you believe it? We'll look at other strategies you can use to deal with anxiety. Until then, have a great week everyone!"

I left her office feeling calm and content. I can't believe group is almost over, but mostly I can't help thinking HOW MUCH BETTER I FEEL!

CHAPTER 6

Follow Up Discussion Questions and Activities

Discussion Questions

1. Do you think everyone could benefit from exercise and journaling to deal with their anxiety?

- Can those strategies make anyone calmer, or just those who have anxiety?

2. Have you tried journaling as a way to deal with anxiety? Have you used it to better understand your thoughts and feelings?

- Did you like journaling?

3. Have you used physical exercise as a way to deal with anxiety? Or have you ever used exercise to deal with emotions, such as frustration, anger, or disappointment?

© 2022 Father Flanagan's Boys' Home

- Did you like exercising?

____

____

____

4. Have you ever noticed a change in your emotions after you've exercised or written in your journal, even if it was part of an assignment or class activity?

____

____

____

5. What strategy do you think you'd enjoy more, physical exercise or journaling?

____

____

____

- Why?

____

____

____

Activities

Journaling Activity

1. Explain to the group: I want you to try journaling. I'm giving you 15 minutes to write about your day. You can either write in complete sentences or short bullet points, however you would journal on your own, don't worry about grammar or punctuation.

2. Allow students 15 minutes to journal.

3. Ask the group: How do you feel after journaling? Is there any change in your mood/emotions?

Time-Management Activity

1. Discuss with the group: Would you prefer journaling or exercising to help reduce stress? How would you incorporate either strategy into your daily routine?

2. Give each student the Time Management Activity Worksheet.

3. Explain to students: On the Time Management Worksheet, block off times in the day based on what you already do and have to do (i.e., school from 8:00-3:00, sleep, extracurricular activities, dinner, etc.). Then, you should add 15 minutes into your daily schedule of either journaling or exercising, whichever one you think will work best for you.

4. Optional: Follow-up a few days later:

    - Have you noticed any changes since adding the stress-reducing strategy of journaling or exercising?
    - Was it easy to find 15 minutes in your day to journal or exercise?
    - What benefits do you hope for or expect to achieve using this strategy?
    - Do you have any concerns about adding an anxiety-reducing strategy to your day?

© 2022 Father Flanagan's Boys' Home

MY ANXIETY IS MESSING THINGS UP

TIME MANAGEMENT ACTIVITY WORKSHEET

How would you incorporate journaling or exercising into your daily routine, add 15 mins for each strategy.

TIME	MONDAY	TUESDAY	WEDNESDAY	THURDAY	FRIDAY	SATURDAY	SUNDAY

TEACHER AND COUNSELOR ACTIVITY GUIDE

Chapter 7

Mrs. Wang offered a warm, enthusiastic welcome as we gathered for our last group meeting. She wasted no time and got right to the heart of the matter.

"Today we'll focus on other strategies you can use to deal with anxiety. When you decide on the strategies you like, you'll need to practice them, even on days you don't feel anxious."

"Regular practice will help lower your anxiety and train your body to respond better during anxious times," explained Mrs. Wang. "Would anyone like to share a new strategy we haven't discussed yet? One you've tried or maybe one you've heard of?" she asked.

No one answered until I spoke up. "My mom told me to listen to relaxing music when I'm trying to fall

ASLEEP. BUT, IT HASN'T REALLY HELPED ME TOO MUCH."

"Yes, relaxing music can calm you during stressful times," agreed Mrs. Wang. "But maybe that strategy alone wasn't enough to combat your anxiety. Often, people need to combine a few strategies to feel a POSITIVE CHANGE. Music is a great strategy, either relaxing music or upbeat music can be used, they're just used differently. For example, some people like dancing to upbeat music when they're anxious. It releases their tension."

"Dancing combines two strategies, physical movement and music. Any time you combine strategies, it can be even more effective. Depending on your mood and personality, you can decide which type of music you want to use."

"I had a counselor tell me to do breathing exercises," said Nia. "But I don't know how that could help?"

"Yes, Nia, deep breathing can be especially helpful in dealing with anxiety. Deep breathing increases oxygen to the brain and promotes calmness. And it's a great strategy because you can use it no matter where you are," said Mrs. Wang.

"LET'S PRACTICE DEEP BREATHING RIGHT NOW."

She asked all of us to breathe in deeply for three seconds, and watch as our stomachs moved outward. Then we had to hold our breath for three seconds before exhaling slowly for another three seconds. Again she wanted us to watch as our stomachs moved inward. We repeated this breathing exercise ten times. When we stopped, I was completely relaxed. I think we all were. It was awesome having another strategy to help me reduce my anxiety.

Before group ended, Mrs. Wang offered us an important piece of advice.

"If your anxiety gets worse or the strategies aren't helping, you should talk to a trusted adult. You can always come to me or you can talk to your teachers, your parents, your coaches, or anyone who cares about you. Sometimes, you may need more support and help, and that's okay. So, please reach out to someone you trust if you need help managing your anxiety."

Long after group ended, I kept practicing the strategies I learned. I journal, ride my bike, and do deep breathing exercises every day. I feel so much calmer when I use all three strategies. When I'm busy and don't spend much time doing any of them, my anxiety creeps back up. I have trouble falling asleep, too.

It didn't take long for me to see what a difference these strategies had on my life. I discovered I can't rely on just one. I need to do them all to deal with my anxiety. I'm sleeping better now, my mood has improved A LOT, and I can control my emotions better. I haven't gotten into any more fights with my friends!

Walking into school this morning, I couldn't help but think of how great it was that I decided to join the CATS Group. I learned how to manage my anxiety and that I wasn't alone. Other kids struggle with it, too. Seeing my friends goofing on each other in their usual spot made me smile.

"Hey Oscar, what's up?" Darius asked me.

"Not much. Just super excited for another day of school," I joked.

"Oscar, you've been unusually happy lately," Jayden said. Then, in all seriousness, he asked, "What's the deal? You been eating some special breakfast or something?"

Everyone burst out laughing. I told the guys it was because I was finally getting enough sleep.

"Glad you're happy," Darius said. "NOW MAYBE WE CAN ALL CHILL OUT AND HAVE FUN!"

I was proud of myself. All the time I spent working on managing my anxiety was paying off. I was feeling good and my friends noticed, too.

I DIDN'T FEEL LIKE I NEEDED TO EXPLAIN ALL THE CHANGES I MADE AND HOW THE CATS GROUP HELPED ME. MAYBE SOMEDAY I WILL. BUT, FOR NOW, I'M GOING TO KEEP MY JOURNEY ON THE DOWN LOW. JUST BETWEEN ME AND THE GANG FROM THE CATS GROUP.

CHAPTER 7

Follow Up Discussion Questions and Activities

Discussion Questions

1. Have you tried breathing exercises to reduce anxiety?

- Did you like this strategy?

2. Have you tried playing music to reduce anxiety?

- What kind of music did you play?
- Did you like this strategy?

3. What anxiety-reducing strategies were discussed in this book?

4. Are there any strategies discussed in this book that you will incorporate into your life?

5. Are there anxiety-reducing strategies that weren't mentioned in the book?

- What strategies were not mentioned?

© 2022 Father Flanagan's Boys' Home

6. Were you surprised to see that Oscar was able to better deal well with his anxiety by the end of the story?

____

____

- Why or why not?

____

7. What differences do you think Oscar's friends see in him (i.e., mood, attitude, behaviors, etc.)?

____

____

8. How do you think Oscar felt when his friends noticed his happier mood?

____

____

- Why do you think that?

____

9. Why do you think Oscar didn't tell his friends about the group?

____

____

- Do you think Oscar should have told his friends about the CATS Group?

____

- Are there any benefits of Oscar telling his friends about the group?

____

- Are there any negative effects of Oscar telling his friends about the group?

____

Activities

Exploring Options Activity

1. Discuss with the group: Oscar is glad he joined the CATS Group. He learned so much. Do you think he did the right thing by joining group?
   - Why or why not?
   - What are other ways Oscar could have helped his anxiety?
2. Write additional options on the board for students to see.
3. Continue discussion: Looking at the options we discussed, which option do you think is best for Oscar?
   - Why?
   - Vote on the best option for Oscar.
4. Divide students into groups, based on the best option they chose for Oscar.
5. Explain: I'm giving each group time to discuss the possible outcomes and consequences if Oscar chooses the option your group thinks is best. How might Oscar's life change, both positively and negatively?
6. Give groups about 15 minutes to discuss the possible outcomes and consequences.
7. Have groups pick a representative to share the possible outcomes and consequences if Oscar chooses the option their group thought was best.
8. Continue discussion:
   - (For the group presenting) Do you still think this is the best option for Oscar after exploring the possible outcomes and consequences?
   - (For the other groups) Has anyone in another group changed their mind about the best option for Oscar?

© 2022 Father Flanagan's Boys' Home

MY ANXIETY IS MESSING THINGS UP

Exploring Questions Activity

1. Ask students: Do you have any additional questions about anxiety after reading the book?
2. Group students into pairs.
3. Instruct students: Discuss with your partner any additional questions you have about anxiety that weren't addressed in the story. Write down any questions and if you don't have any questions, discuss what you learned about anxiety from the story.
4. Give students time to discuss what they learned about anxiety and any questions they still have about anxiety.
5. Ask students: Would any partner groups like to share what you discussed?

Boys Town Press books

Kid-friendly books for teaching social skills

A book series and accompanying activity guides focused on changing friendships, finding your place, advocating for yourself, and being true to who you are.

978-1-944882-63-1

978-1-944882-64-8

978-1-944882-65-5

978-1-944882-66-2

978-1-944882-67-9

978-1-944882-68-6

978-1-944882-89-1

978-1-944882-90-7

Jennifer Licate
GRADES 4-8

A book series teaching important lessons about lying, cheating, and being a good friend.

BoysTownPress.org

For information on Boys Town, its Education Model®, Common Sense Parenting®, and training programs:
boystowntraining.org, boystown.org/parenting
training@BoysTown.org, 1-800-545-5771

For parenting and educational books and other resources:
BoysTownPress.org, btpress@BoysTown.org, 1-800-282-6657